50 Classic Poems Every Boy Should Know

50 Classic Poems Every Boy Should Know

WELKIN BOOKS

for Caradoc

First Published 2015
Welkin Books Ltd

Copyright © Welkin Books Ltd 2015
Translations on p13 & p15 Copyright © Thor Ewing 2015
Thor Ewing asserts his right to be identified as author and illustrator in accordance with the Design, Copyrights and Patents Act 1988

All rights reserved. No part of this publication may be reproduced, stored in a retrieval system, or transmitted in any form or by any means, without the prior written permission of the publisher, nor be otherwise circulated in any from of binding or cover other than that in which it is published and without a similar condition being imposed upon the subsequent purchaser.

ISBN 978-1-910075-03-6

Foreword

The poems in this book have all been chosen for boys and young men from among the countless poems composed in the English language over the last thousand years of our history. Many of them are poems which I read as a boy myself, and which still inspire me today. But although these poems have been chosen with boys in mind, that doesn't mean they were written just for boys. If a poem works, it can work for anyone, boy or girl, no matter what age they are.

Some of the poems in this collection are about war and battles. Of course, we don't all grow up to be soldiers, but the values which men have fought by in the past are also valuable in other walks of life. Heroism means standing up for what you know to be right and good, no matter what. So, it's not only on the battlefield that you'll find heroes.

Many poems are not about war and adventure. Other poems in the collection explore other aspects of life, what it is to be alive and what it takes to lead a full life.

There is also a brief word about each of the poets and their poems, and there are occasional notes to explain some of the more unusual words and references.

T. E.

Contents

The Battle of Maldon, AD 991	12
Byrhtwold's Speech	13
Armourers at work, c.1350	14
Swarthy, Smoky Smiths	15
John Barbour, c.1320–95	16
Ah! Freedom is a Noble Thing	17
Geoffrey Chaucer, c.1343 – 1400	18
A Knyght Ther Was	19
Sir Walter Raleigh, c.1552 – 1618	20
Cowards Fear to Die	21
William Shakespeare, 1564 – 1616	22
Fear No More the Heat o' the Sun	23
John Dryden, 1631–1700	24
Happy the Man	25
Anne Finch, Countess of Winchilsea, 1661 – 1720	26
The Fallen Soldier	27
William Blake, 1757 – 1827	28
The Tyger	29
And Did those Feet in Ancient Time	30
Robert Burns, 1759–96	31
Bannockburn	32
A Man's a Man for A' That	34
James Hogg, 1770 – 1835	36
A Boy's Song	37
Thomas Love Peacock, 1785 – 1866	39
The War Song of Dinas Vawr	40

George Gordon, Lord Byron, 1788 - 1824	42
The Destruction of Sennacherib	43
Charles Wolfe, 1791 - 1823	45
The Burial of Sir John Moore after Corunna	46
Percy Bysshe Shelley, 1792 - 1822	48
Ozymandias	49
Felicia Dorothea Hemans, 1793 - 1835	50
Casabianca	51
John Keats, 1795 - 1821	53
La Belle Dame sans Merci	54
Henry Wadsworth Longfellow, 1807-82	57
The Witnesses	58
A Psalm of Life	60
John Greenleaf Whittier, 1807-92	62
Barbara Frietchie	63
Frances Anne Kemble, 1809-93	66
The Wreck of the Birkenhead	67
Alfred, Lord Tennyson, 1809-92	72
The Charge of the Light Brigade	73
The *Revenge*	75
Robert Browning, 1812-89	80
An Incident of the French Camp	81
Robert Traill Spence Lowell, 1816-91	83
The Relief of Lucknow	84
Arthur Hugh Clough, 1819-61	88
Say not the Struggle Nought Availeth	89
Charles Kingsley, 1819-75	90
Young and Old	91

Herman Melville, 1819-91	92
Malvern Hill	93
Christina Rossetti, 1830-94	95
Remember	96
Thomas Hardy, 1840 - 1928	97
Heredity	98
In Time of 'The Breaking of Nations'	99
Gerard Manley Hopkins, 1844-89	100
Inversnaid	101
Felix Randal	102
Thomas Armstrong, 1848 - 1919	103
The Trimdon Grange Explosion	104
William Ernest Henley, 1849 - 1903	106
Invictus	107
Robert Louis Stevenson, 1850-94	108
Where Go the Boats?	109
Ticonderoga	110
Sir Henry Newbolt, 1862 - 1938	121
Vitaï Lampada	122
Drake's Drum	123
Rudyard Kipling, 1865 - 1936	124
If—	125
The Way through the Woods	127
Henry Lawson, 1867 - 1922	128
The Glass on the Bar	129
W. H. Davies, 1871 - 1940	131
Leisure	132
Paul Laurence Dunbar, 1872 - 1906	133
Sympathy	134

Edward Thomas, 1878 - 1917	135
Adlestrop	136
James Elroy Flecker, 1884 - 1915	137
The Old Ships	138
Rupert Brooke, 1887 - 1915	140
The Soldier	141
Wilfred Owen, 1893 - 1918	142
Futility	143

The Battle of Maldon, AD 991

These lines describe a disastrous Anglo-Saxon battle against Viking attackers, which was fought at Maldon, Essex, in 991 AD. The Anglo-Saxon leader, Byrhtnoth, Ealdorman of Essex, had agreed to allow the Vikings ashore so he could bring them to battle. In the fighting which followed, Byrhtnoth was killed and the Anglo-Saxons were defeated. Byrhtnoth's bodyguard refused to leave his side after his death, and stood their ground until they too were killed. Some time afterwards, a poem was written to commemorate Byrhtnoth and his men, and 350 lines of this poem survive on a fragment of Anglo-Saxon manuscript. This passage describes how Byrhtwold, one of Byrhtnoth's warriors, rallied the men before their last stand.

Byrhtwold's Speech

THEN Byrhtwold spoke out, his shield held aloft,
The hard-bitten henchman, shaking his spear shaft,
With words of bravery he emboldened the warband:

 "Thought must be the harder, heart the keener,
Spirit must be the greater as our strength is lessening.
Here lies our leader, cut down before us,
His goodness in the dust. You'll always regret it
If you turn away from this war-play now!
I am wise in this world; I will not go,
But here by the side of my fallen lord,
By the well-loved man, I mean to lie."

from 'The Battle of Maldon'
Anonymous, c.1000AD
Modern English by Thor Ewing

Armourers at work, c.1350

Most medieval poetry is anonymous, which simply means we don't know who wrote it. The medieval landscape would usually have been quiet and tranquil, but this poem vividly expresses the poet's frustration at the constant noise from the hammering of armourers working day and night. Armourers were skilled metal workers, whose work supplied armies for England's wars in Wales, Scotland and France.

Swarthy, Smoky Smiths

SWARTHY, smoky smiths, besmirched with soot,
Drive me to death with the din of their dents.
Such noise of a night, men never have heard,
Such cries of knaves and clattering of knocks;
The crook-backed creatures call for 'Coal, coal!'
And blow at their bellows, till their brains fairly burst.

'Huff puff!' says the one, 'Haff paff!' the other;
They spit and they sprawl, and they tell many tales;
They gnaw and they gnash, and they groan together,
And hold themselves hot with their hard hammers;
Of bull's leather are their long aprons
To shield their shanks from the fiery showers.

Heavy hammers they have, that are hard in the handle;
Strong strokes they strike on a steel stock:
Luss buss! Lass dass! taking their turns
Such a doleful din—may the devil dispel it!
The master lengthens a little bit, and links on a lesser,
Twines them together, and sings out a treble:

Tick tack! Hick hack! Ticket tacket! Tick tack!
Luss buss! Lass dass! such a life do they lead,
All these armourers—may Christ send them sorrow!
That no man for burn-waters at night may take rest.

Anonymous, c.1350AD
Modern English by Thor Ewing

John Barbour, c.1320–95

John Barbour was probably born in south west Scotland, but little is known of his life before adulthood. After serving as a priest at the Cathedral of Dunkeld, he became archdeacon of Aberdeen in 1356. He later worked for King Robert II (1371–90) the first of the Stewart kings. It was while working at the royal court that Barbour wrote his long poem The Brus, which celebrates the life of King Robert the Bruce (1306–29).

These lines in praise of freedom are from the first book of The Brus.

par coeur: *French, 'by heart'*

Ah, Freedom is a Noble Thing!

AH, Freedom is a noble thing!
Freedom makes man to have liking;
Freedom all solace to man gives;
He lives at ease that freely lives!
A noble heart may have none ease,
Nor else nought that may him please,
If freedom fail, for free liking
Is yearned o'er all other thing.
Nor he, that aye has lived free,
May not know well the property,
The anger, nor the wretched doom,
That is coupled to foul thraldom.
But, if he had assayed it,
Then all *par coeur* he should it wit,
And should think freedom more to prize
Than all the gold in world that is.

from The Brus
John Barbour, c.1320-95
Spelling has been modernised

Geoffrey Chaucer, c.1343 – 1400

Geoffrey Chaucer was the son of John Chaucer, a London wine merchant. At the age of 14, he became a page to Elizabeth de Burgh, Countess of Ulster, whose husband Lionel, Duke of Clarence, was the son of King Edward III. Two years later, he went to France with Duke Lionel as part of the English army in the Hundred Years' War. Chaucer was captured by the French at the Siege of Reims, and his ransom was paid by the king. His first major poem was written for Duke Lionel's brother, John of Gaunt, in memory of his young wife Blanche of Lancaster who died in 1369.

Chaucer's longest and most famous work is The Canterbury Tales, *in which a group of pilgrims swap stories to pass the time on their journey from London to Canterbury. These lines from the* General Prologue *to* The Canterbury Tales *introduce a knight as one of the pilgrims.*

A Knyght Ther Was

A KNYGHT ther was, and that a worthy man,
That fro the tyme that he first began
To riden out, he loved chivalrye,
Trouthe, honour, freedom and curtesye.
Ful worthy was he in his lordes warre,
And thereto hadde he riden no man farre,
As wel in Christendom as in heathenesse,
And ever honoured for his worthynesse.

from the General Prologue *to* The Canterbury Tales
Geoffrey Chaucer, c.1343 – 1400

Sir Walter Raleigh, c.1552 - 1618

Walter Raleigh was born in Devon where his father, also named Walter Raleigh, was a Protestant landowner. Protestants were persecuted in England during the reign of the Catholic Queen Mary, and Raleigh's father once had to hide in a church tower to save his life. At the age of just 15, Raleigh went to fight alongside fellow Protestants in France and, in 1580, he fought in Ireland against the Gerald FitzGerald, Earl of Desmond. He was rewarded by Queen Elizabeth I with lands in Ireland, and became a favourite with the queen. He was knighted in 1585, and became Captain of the Queen's Guard in 1587. But the queen was furious when she found he had secretly married one of her ladies-in-waiting, and the couple were imprisoned in the Tower of London until Raleigh succeeded in paying for their release. Between 1595 and 1597, he sailed to Guayana, Cadiz and the Azores. After the death of Queen Elizabeth, Raleigh was accused of plotting against King James I and sentenced to death, but he was released for a final expedition to Guayana where he hoped to find gold to satisfy the king. He returned without gold and was executed. His wife had his head enbalmed, and carried it with her until she died.

Of the many poems by Raleigh, this brief couplet composed the night before his execution is probably the pithiest.

Cowards Fear to Die
On the Snuff of a Candle the Night before he died

>COWARDS fear to die; but courage stout,
>Rather than live in snuff, will be put out.

>>*Sir Walter Raleigh, c.1552 – 1618*

William Shakespeare, 1564 – 1616

William Shakespeare was the son of John Shakespeare, a glovemaker and alderman in Stratford-upon-Avon, Staffordshire. By 1592, he was making his mark as an actor and playwright in London. As well as his theatrical career, Shakespeare also published poetry; his first long poem was published in 1593. Most of his plays were only properly published after his death, in an edition of 1623 known as the First Folio. *Today Shakespeare's plays and poems are known across the world, and he is England's most celebrated writer.*

The poem 'Fear No More the Heat of the Sun' is the lyric of a funeral song in Shakespeare's play Cymbeline, *Act IV, Scene ii.*

Fear No More the Heat o' the Sun

FEAR no more the heat o' the sun,
    Nor the furious winter's rages;
Thou thy worldly task hast done,
    Home art gone, and ta'en thy wages.
Golden lads and girls all must,
As chimney-sweepers, come to dust.

Fear no more the frown o' the great;
    Thou art past the tyrants stroke;
Care no more to clothe and eat;
    To thee the reed is as the oak.
The sceptre, learning, physic, must
All follow this, and come to dust.

Fear no more the lightning flash,
    Nor th' all-dreaded thunder stone;
Fear not slander, censure rash;
    Thou hast finished joy and moan.
All lovers young, all lovers must
Consign to thee, and come to dust.

from Cymbeline, *Act IV, Scene ii*
William Shakespeare, 1564 – 1616

John Dryden, 1631 – 1700

John Dryden was born in Aldwincle, Northamptonshire, where his grandfather was a clergyman, and spent his young boyhood in nearby Titchmarsh. At the age of 13, he was sent to Westminster School and when, six years later, he went on to Cambridge University he had already published his first poem. He worked for the government of Oliver Cromwell, and in 1658 he published a poem in honour of Cromwell, but two years later another poem celebrated the Restoration of the monarchy. As well as writing poetry, Dryden was also well known as a writer of plays and essays.

Dryden's poem 'Happy the Man' is his translation of a poem by the Roman poet Horace. Dryden always translated very freely, saying he wanted to write the poem that the original author would have written 'if he were living and an Englishman.'

Happy the Man

HAPPY the man, and happy he alone,
   He who can call today his own:
   He who, secure within, can say,
"Tomorrow do thy worst, for I have lived today.
   Be fair or foul, or rain or shine,
The joys I have possessed, in spite of fate, are mine.
   Not Heaven itself upon the past has power,
But what has been has been, and I have had my hour."

John Dryden, 1631-1700

Anne Finch, Countess of Winchilsea, 1661 – 1720

Anne Finch was born as Anne Kingsmill, the daughter of Sir William Kingsmill and Anne Haslewood. In 1682, she became a Maid of Honour to Mary of Modena, Duchess of York, at St James's Palace. There she met her future husband Heneage Finch, who was a courtier of James Stuart, Duke of York (later King James II & VII). Anne became Countess of Winchilsea when her husband inherited the title Earl of Winchilsea in 1712. Her first book of poems was published anonymously in 1691. She was concerned that it would not be thought proper for a lady to write and publish her own poetry, and it was not until 1713 that she gave permission for her name to appear.

This passage from her long poem All is Vanity, *denounces the pursuit of honour and glory through war.*

The Fallen Soldier

TRAIL all your pikes, dispirit every drum,
   March in a slow procession from afar,
   Ye silent, ye dejected men of war!
Be still the hautboys, and the flute be dumb!

Display no more, in vain, the loftly banner.
   For see! where on the bier before ye lies
   The pale, the fall'n th' untimely sacrifice
To your mistaken shrine, to your false idol Honour!

from All is Vanity
Anne Finch, Countess of Winchilsea, 1661 - 1720

William Blake, 1757 – 1827

William Blake grew up above his father's hosiery shop in London's Soho, and left school at the age of 10. In 1772, Blake was apprenticed as an engraver, preparing drawings for print. It is chiefly as an artist and engraver that he is remembered today. During his lifetime Blake's poetry was only published in very limited editions, and just forty copies of his first book of poems were printed in 1783.

Blake's poem 'The Tyger' evokes the animal in all its beauty and ferocity.

His poem 'And Did those Feet in Ancient Time' has become famous as the lyric of the song 'Jerusalem.' It refers to an old legend that the young Jesus was once brought to England by his great uncle Joseph of Arimathea.

The Tyger

TYGER, Tyger, burning bright,
In the forests of the night;
What immortal hand or eye,
Could frame thy fearful symmetry?

In what distant deeps or skies
Burnt the fire of thine eyes?
On what wings dare he aspire?
What the hand, dare seize the fire?

And what shoulder, & what art,
Could twist the sinews of thy heart?
And when thy heart began to beat,
What dread hand? & what dread feet?

What the hammer? what the chain,
In what furnace was thy brain?
What the anvil? what dread grasp,
Dare its deadly terrors clasp!

When the stars threw down their spears
And water'd heaven with their tears:
Did he smile his work to see?
Did he who made the Lamb make thee?

Tyger, Tyger burning bright,
In the forests of the night:
What immortal hand or eye,
Dare frame thy fearful symmetry?

William Blake, 1757 - 1827

And Did those Feet in Ancient Time

AND did those feet in ancient time
Walk upon England's mountains green?
And was the holy Lamb of God
On England's pleasant pastures seen?

And did the Countenance Divine
Shine forth upon our clouded hills?
And was Jerusalem builded here
Among these dark Satanic Mills?

Bring me my bow of burning gold!
Bring me my arrows of desire!
Bring me my spear! O clouds, unfold!
Bring me my chariot of fire!

I will not cease from mental fight,
Nor shall my sword sleep in my hand,
Till we have built Jerusalem
In England's green and pleasant land.

William Blake, 1757 - 1827

Robert Burns, 1759-96

Robert Burns was born in the house his father built in Alloway, Ayrshire. The family moved to a nearby farm when Burns was 7 years old and, by the age of 15, he was doing most of the work on the farm. In 1786, Burns decided to emigrate to Jamaica, and published a book of poems to pay for the trip. This book, which was written 'chiefly in the Scottish dialect,' was so successful that Burns decided to stay. Robert Burns is now regarded as Scotland's national poet, and his birthday is still marked every year as Burns Night.

In his poem 'Bannockburn,' Burns imagines the speech which King Robert Bruce gave to his soldiers in 1314 before the battle against English forces led by King Edward II.

In 'A Man's a Man for A' That,' Burns hopes for a future where all people will be equal, and where the inner qualities of virtue and honesty will count for more than outward show of wealth and rank.

Bannockburn

AT Bannockburn the English lay,—
The Scots they were na far away,
But waited for the break o' day
    That glinted in the east.

But soon the sun broke through the heath
And lighted up that field of death,
When Bruce, wi' saul-inspiring breath,
    His heralds thus addressed:—

"Scots, wha hae wi' Wallace bled,
Scots, wham Bruce has aften led;
Welcome to your gory bed,
    Or to Victory!

"Now's the day, and now's the hour;
See the front o' battle lour;
See approach proud Edward's power—
    Chains and Slavery!

"Wha will be a traitor knave?
Wha can fill a coward's grave!
Wha sae base as be a slave?
    Let him turn and flee!

"Wha for Scotland's king and law
Freedom's sword will strongly draw,
Freeman stand, or Freeman fa',
   Let him follow me!

"By Oppression's woes and pains!
By your sons in servile chains!
We will drain our dearest veins,
   But they shall be free!

"Lay the proud usurpers low!
Tyrants fall in every foe!
Liberty's in every blow!—
   Let us do or die!"

Robert Burns, 1759-96

A Man's a Man for A' That

IS there for honest Poverty
   That hings his head, an' a' that;
The coward slave—we pass him by,
   We dare be poor for a' that!
For a' that, an' a' that.
   Our toils obscure an' a' that,
The rank is but the guinea's stamp,
   The Man's the gowd for a' that.

What though on hamely fare we dine,
   Wear hoddin grey, an' a that;
Gie fools their silks, and knaves their wine;
   A Man's a Man for a' that:
For a' that, an' a' that,
   Their tinsel show, an' a' that;
The honest man, tho' e'er sae poor,
   Is king o' men for a' that.

Ye see yon birkie, ca'd a lord,
   Wha struts, an' stares, an' a' that;
Tho' hundreds worship at his word,
   He's but a coof for a' that:
For a' that, an' a' that,
   His ribband, star, an' a' that:
The man o' independent mind
   He looks an' laughs at a' that.

A prince can mak a belted knight,
    A marquis, duke, an' a' that;
But an honest man's aboon his might,
    Gude faith, he maunna fa' that!
For a' that, an' a' that,
    Their dignities an' a' that;
The pith o' sense, an' pride o' worth,
    Are higher rank than a' that.

Then let us pray that come it may,
    (As come it will for a' that,)
That Sense and Worth, o'er a' the earth,
    Shall bear the gree, an' a' that.
For a' that, an' a' that,
    It's coming yet for a' that,
That Man to Man, the world o'er,
    Shall brothers be for a' that.

Robert Burns, 1759-96

James Hogg, 1770 – 1835

James Hogg was the son of a tenant farmer in Ettrick in the Scottish Borders. His grandfather is said to have been the last man ever to speak with the fairies. Hogg's father lost money as a farmer and took a job as a shepherd, and Hogg worked as a farm servant for most of his childhood. At the age of 18 he too became a shepherd, and he used his time tending sheep as a chance to learn to read. He published his first book of poems in 1801, and some years later Hogg moved to Edinburgh to live as a writer. Several of Hogg's works achieved success but, despite his talent, Hogg found real difficulties breaking into Edinburgh's literary world. Among his admirers was the Duke of Buccleuch, who granted him a small farm where he could live rent free.

Hogg's poem 'A Boy's Song' looks back on childhood days spent playing in the countryside with his older brother Billy.

A Boy's Song

WHERE the pools are bright and deep,
Where the grey trout lies asleep,
Up the river and over the lea,
That's the way for Billy and me.

Where the blackbird sings the latest,
Where the hawthorn blooms the sweetest,
Where the nestlings chirp and flee,
That's the way for Billy and me.

Where the mowers mow the cleanest,
Where the hay lies thick and greenest,
There to track the homeward bee,
That's the way for Billy and me.

Where the hazel bank is steepest,
Where the shadow falls the deepest,
Where the clustering nuts fall free,
That's the way for Billy and me.

Why the boys should drive away
Little sweet maidens from their play,
Or love to banter and fight so well,
That's the thing I never could tell.

But this I know, I love to play
Through the meadow, among the hay;
Up the water and over the lea,
That's the way for Billy and me.

James Hogg, 1770 – 1835

Thomas Love Peacock, 1785 – 1866

Thomas Love Peacock grew up in Chertsey, Surrey. His father, a London glass merchant, died when Thomas was 9 years old. He worked as a clerk in London and later as a secretary on board HMS Venerable. He was fond of walking, and he toured Scotland, Wales and the Thames Valley on foot. In 1819, he began work for the East India Company, which at that time ruled much of India. Peacock became well known as a writer of satirical novels. He published his first book of poetry in 1804.

Peacock published his poem 'The War Song of Dinas Vawr' in a comic novel, which doesn't take the exploits of its warrior heroes terribly seriously. Ednyfed is the legendary founder of the royal line of Dyfed.

meeter: *more fitting*
kine: *cattle*

The War Song of Dinas Vawr

THE mountain sheep are sweeter,
But the valley sheep are fatter;
We therefore deemed it meeter
To carry off the latter.
We made an expedition;
We met a host, and quelled it;
We forced a strong position,
And killed the men who held it.

On Dyfed's richest valley,
Where herds of kine were browsing,
We made a mighty sally,
To furnish our carousing.
Fierce warriors rushed to meet us;
We met them, and o'erthrew them:
They struggled hard to beat us;
But we conquered them, and slew them.

As we drove our prize at leisure,
The king marched forth to catch us:
His rage surpassed all measure,
But his people could not match us.
He fled to his hall-pillars;
And, ere our force we led off,
Some sacked his house and cellars,
While others cut his head off.

We there, in strife bewild'ring,
Spilt blood enough to swim in:
We orphaned many children,
And widowed many women.
The eagles and the ravens
We glutted with our foemen;
The heroes and the cravens,
The spearmen and the bowmen.

We brought away from battle,
And much their land bemoaned them,
Two thousand head of cattle,
And the head of him who owned them:
Ednyfed, king of Dyfed,
His head was borne before us;
His wine and beasts supplied our feasts,
And his overthrow, our chorus.

Thomas Love Peacock, 1785 - 1866

George Gordon, Lord Byron, 1788 – 1824

George Gordon was the son of John 'Mad Jack' Byron, a captain in the Coldstream Guards, and Catherine Gordon. His mother was heir to lands and money in Aberdeenshire, but by the time George was born his father had already spent her money and left to live in France. The young Byron grew up in Aberdeen, and at the age of 10 he inherited the title Lord Byron from his father's uncle, who had been known as 'the Wicked' Lord Byron. He went to Harrow School and to Cambridge University, where he kept a pet bear. Byron spent much of his adult life in Europe, sometimes led by his unending succession of scandalous love affairs. In 1823, Byron joined the struggle for Greek independence, paying for the refitting of the Greek fleet and planning an attack on Greece's Ottoman overlords. He fell ill and died at Missolonghi, Greece, before his expedition set sail.

Byron's poem 'The Destruction of Sennacherib' evocatively recounts the Biblical story of the Assyrian King Sennacherib's siege of Jerusalem, where the Angel of the Lord is said to have put to death 185,000 Assyrian troops as they slept (II Kings 19:35). Contemporary Assyrian accounts of the same event in 701 BC tell a very different story.

The Destruction of Sennacherib

THE Assyrian came down like the wolf on the fold,
And his cohorts were gleaming in purple and gold;
And the sheen of their spears was like stars on the sea,
When the blue wave rolls nightly on deep Galilee.

Like the leaves of the forest when Summer is green,
That host with their banners at sunset were seen:
Like the leaves of the forest when Autumn hath blown,
That host on the morrow lay withered and strown.

For the Angel of Death spread his wings on the blast,
And breathed in the face of the foe as he passed;
And the eyes of the sleepers waxed deadly and chill,
And their hearts but once heaved, and for ever grew still!

And there lay the steed with his nostril all wide,
But through it there rolled not the breath of his pride;
And the foam of his gasping lay white on the turf,
And cold as the spray of the rock-beating surf.

And there lay the rider distorted and pale,
With the dew on his brow, and the rust on his mail:
And the tents were all silent, the banners alone,
The lances unlifted, the trumpet unblown.

And the widows of Ashur are loud in their wail,
And the idols are broke in the temple of Baal;
And the might of the Gentile, unsmote by the sword,
Hath melted like snow in the glance of the Lord!

George Gordon, Lord Byron, 1788 - 1824

Charles Wolfe, 1791 – 1823

Charles Wolfe was born into a landowning family from County Kildare, but his father died shortly after he was born and he moved with his mother to England where he grew up. He returned to Ireland to study at Trinity College, Dublin, and became a Church of Ireland clergyman. Wolfe died of consumption in Cobh, Co. Cork, at the age of 31.

Wolfe's poem 'The Burial of Sir John Moore after Corunna' describes an incident in the Napoleonic Wars. In 1809, Sir John Moore, the British commander in Spain, ordered his army to retreat in the face of a superior French force. Moore headed for the ports of Vigo and Corunna where his troops could embark for England but, rather than board their ships as planned, the British were forced to hold off a French attack. While rallying his troops, Moore was hit by a cannonball. He later died of his wounds, but lived long enough to know that his action had been successful. The British soldiers buried their leader's body, before leaving under cover of night.

The Burial of Sir John Moore after Corunna

NOT a drum was heard, not a funeral note,
    As his corse to the rampart we hurried;
Not a soldier discharged his farewell shot
    O'er the grave where our hero we buried.

We buried him darkly at dead of night,
    The sods with our bayonets turning,
By the struggling moonbeam's misty light
    And the lanthorn dimly burning.

No useless coffin enclosed his breast,
    Not in sheet or in shroud we wound him;
But he lay like a warrior taking his rest
    With his martial cloak around him.

Few and short were the prayers we said,
    And we spoke not a word of sorrow;
But we steadfastly gazed on the face that was dead,
    And we bitterly thought of the morrow.

We thought, as we hollow'd his narrow bed
    And smooth'd down his lonely pillow,
That the foe and the stranger would tread o'er his head,
    And we far away on the billow!

Lightly they'll talk of the spirit that's gone,
    And o'er his cold ashes upbraid him—
But little he'll reck, if they let him sleep on
    In the grave where a Briton has laid him.

But half of our heavy task was done
    When the clock struck the hour for retiring;
And we heard the distant and random gun
    That the foe was sullenly firing.

Slowly and sadly we laid him down,
    From the field of his fame fresh and gory;
We carved not a line, and we raised not a stone,
    But we left him alone with his glory.

Charles Wolfe, 1791 – 1823

Percy Bysshe Shelley, 1792 – 1822

Shelley was the son of the MP for Horsham, Sussex, where he was born. He went to school at Eton and then to Oxford University. In 1810, Shelley co-authored two books of poetry, both of which were published under false identities. Shelley was expelled from university and almost immediately eloped to Scotland where he married Harriet Westbrook, a schoolfriend of his sisters. However in 1814, he left Harriet to run off with Mary Godwin, and the couple married after Shelley's first wife committed suicide—Mary Shelley would also achieve fame as the writer of the novel Frankenstein. *From 1818, the Shelleys lived in Italy, where Shelley was drowned in a storm at sea in 1822. When his body was found after 11 days, he was cremated on the beach. A friend plucked his heart from the funeral pyre and gave it to Mary Shelley, who kept it for the rest of her life.*

When Shelley's poem 'Ozymandius' was written, the head of an immense stone statue of the Ancient Egyptian pharaoh Ozymandius (Rameses II, 1279-13 BC) was on its way to London, where it is still displayed in the British Museum.

Ozymandias

I MET a traveller from an antique land
Who said: Two vast and trunkless legs of stone
Stand in the desert... Near them, on the sand,
Half sunk, a shattered visage lies, whose frown,
And wrinkled lip, and sneer of cold command,
Tell that its sculptor well those passions read
Which yet survive, stamped on these lifeless things,
That hand that mocked them and the heart that fed;
And on the pedestal these words appear:
'My name is OZYMANDIAS, king of kings:
Look on my works, ye Mighty, and despair!'
Nothing beside remains. Round the decay
Of that colossal wreck, boundless and bare
The lone and level sands stretch far away.

Percy Bysshe Shelley, 1792 – 1822

Felicia Dorothea Hemans, 1793 – 1835

Felicia Hemans was born as Felicia Browne, the daughter of a Liverpool wine importer, and she grew up in North Wales. Her first book of poems was published in 1808 when she was just 14. In 1812, Felicia married the Irish army officer Capt. Alfred Hemans. She became widely renowned as a writer. Felicia Hemans died in at her home in Dublin at the age of 41.

'Casabianca' commemorates an incident at the Battle of the Nile in 1798, when the British fleet under Admiral Nelson sought out and destroyed Napoleon's French fleet, leaving the French army marooned in Egypt. The French ship Orient was destroyed in a massive explosion, killing its captain Louis de Casabianca and his 12-year-old son Giocante.

Casabianca

THE boy stood on the burning deck
    Whence all but he had fled;
The flame that lit the battle's wreck
    Shone round him o'er the dead.

Yet beautiful and bright he stood,
    As born to rule the storm;
A creature of heroic blood,
    A proud, though childlike form.

The flames rolled on—he would not go
    Without his father's word;
That father, faint in death below,
    His voice no longer heard.

He called aloud—"Say, father, say,
    If yet my task is done?"
He knew not that the chieftain lay
    Unconscious of his son.

"Speak, father!" once again he cried,
    "If I may yet be gone!"
And but the booming shots replied,
    And fast the flames rolled on.

Upon his brow he felt their breath,
   And in his waving hair,
And looked from that lone post of death
   In still, yet brave despair.

And shouted but once more aloud,
   "My father! must I stay?"
While o'er him fast, through sail and shroud,
   The wreathing fires made way.

They wrapt the ship in splendour wild,
   They caught the flag on high,
And streamed above the gallant child,
   Like banners in the sky.

There came a burst of thunder sound—
   The boy—oh! where was he?
Ask of the winds that far around
   With fragments strewed the sea!—

With mast, and helm, and pennon fair
   That well had borne their part—
But the noblest thing that perished there
   Was that young, faithful heart.

Felicia Dorothea Hemans, 1793 - 1835

John Keats, 1795 – 1821

John Keats was born in Moorgate, London, where his father was an ostler taking care of horses at the Swan and Hoop Inn (now The Globe). His father died after a riding accident when Keats was 8 years old, and his mother died when he was 14. Keats trained as a surgeon and he worked and studied at Guy's Hospital, but he was more and more drawn to poetry. He published his first book of poems in 1816. Keats became sick with tuberculosis after nursing his dying brother and, in 1820, he moved to Rome on the advice of his doctors. When he died in 1821, Keats was just 25 years old. Believing that his poetic career had been a failure, Keats asked for his gravestone to be inscribed, 'Here lies one whose name was writ in water.' It was only after his death that his poetry became famous.

His poem 'La Belle Dame sans Merci' (The Beautiful Lady without Mercy) is a powerful but enigmatic exploration of the themes of Love and Death.

La Belle Dame sans Merci: A Ballad

"O WHAT can ail thee, knight-at-arms,
    Alone and palely loitering?
The sedge has withered from the lake,
    And no birds sing.

"O what can ail thee, knight-at-arms,
    So haggard and so woe-begone?
The squirrel's granary is full,
    And the harvest's done.

"I see a lily on thy brow,
    With anguish moist and fever-dew,
And on thy cheeks a fading rose
    Fast withereth too.

"I met a lady in the meads,
    Full beautiful—a faery's child,
Her hair was long, her foot was light,
    And her eyes were wild.

"I made a garland for her head,
    And bracelets too, and fragrant zone;
She looked at me as she did love,
    And made sweet moan

"I set her on my pacing steed,
    And nothing else saw all day long,
For sidelong would she bend, and sing
    A faery's song.

"She found me roots of relish sweet,
    And honey wild, and manna-dew,
And sure in language strange she said—
    'I love thee true'.

"She took me to her Elfin grot,
    And there she wept and sighed full sore,
And there I shut her wild wild eyes
    With kisses four.

"And there she lullèd me asleep,
    And there I dreamed—Ah! woe betide!—
The latest dream I ever dreamt
    On the cold hill side.

"I saw pale kings and princes too,
    Pale warriors, death-pale were they all;
They cried—'La Belle Dame sans Merci
    Thee hath in thrall!'

"I saw their starved lips in the gloam,
   With horrid warning gapèd wide,
And I awoke and found me here,
   On the cold hill's side.

"And this is why I sojourn here,
   Alone and palely loitering,
Though the sedge is withered from the lake,
   And no birds sing."

John Keats, 1795 – 1821

Henry Wadsworth Longfellow, 1807–82

Longfellow was born in the city of Portland, Maine, in America, where his father was a lawyer. His father was also a trustee of Bowdoin College, where Longfellow studied and later worked as an academic. He published his first book of poems in 1839, and his poetry quickly became popular. Today he is best known for his epic poem Hiawatha.

Longfellow's poem 'The Witnesses' imagines the bones of drowned slaves on the sea-bed bearing witness to the inhumanity of slavery.

'A Psalm of Life' is Longfellow's spirited answer to more negative views of what it is to be alive.

The Witnesses

IN Ocean's wide domains,
    Half buried in the sands,
Lie skeletons in chains,
    With shackled feet and hands.

Beyond the fall of dews,
    Deeper than plummet lies,
Float ships, with all their crews,
    No more to sink nor rise.

There the black Slave-ship swims,
    Freighted with human forms,
Whose fettered, fleshless limbs
    Are not the sport of storms.

These are the bones of Slaves;
    They gleam from the abyss;
They cry, from yawning waves,
    "We are the Witnesses!"

Within Earth's wide domains
    Are markets for men's lives;
Their necks are galled with chains,
    Their wrists are cramped with gyves.

Dead bodies, that the kite
   In deserts makes its prey;
Murders, that with affright
   Scare school-boys from their play!

All evil thoughts and deeds;
   Anger, and lust, and pride;
The foulest, rankest weeds,
   That choke Life's groaning tide!

These are the woes of Slaves;
   They glare from the abyss;
They cry, from unknown graves,
   "We are the Witnesses!"

Henry Wadsworth Longfellow, 1807–82

A Psalm of Life

What the Heart of the Young Man said to the Psalmist.

    TELL me not, in mournful numbers,
        Life is but an empty dream!
    For the soul is dead that slumbers,
        And things are not what they seem.

    Life is real! Life is earnest!
        And the grave is not its goal;
    Dust thou art, to dust returnest,
        Was not spoken of the soul.

    Not enjoyment, and not sorrow,
        Is our destined end or way;
    But to act, that each to-morrow
        Find us farther than to-day.

    Art is long, and Time is fleeting,
        And our hearts, though stout and brave,
    Still, like muffled drums, are beating
        Funeral marches to the grave.

    In the world's broad field of battle,
        In the bivouac of Life,
    Be not like dumb, driven cattle!
        Be a hero in the strife!

Trust no Future, howe'er pleasant!
    Let the dead Past bury its dead!
Act,— act in the living Present!
    Heart within, and God o'erhead!

Lives of great men all remind us
    We can make our lives sublime,
And, departing, leave behind us
    Footprints on the sands of time;

Footprints, that perhaps another,
    Sailing o'er life's solemn main,
A forlorn and shipwrecked brother,
    Seeing, shall take heart again.

Let us, then, be up and doing,
    With a heart for any fate;
Still achieving, still pursuing,
    Learn to labor and to wait.

Henry Wadsworth Longfellow, 1807–82

John Greenleaf Whittier, 1807-92

John Greenleaf Whittier was born on a farm in Massachusetts, America. He worked as a shoemaker to help pay his school fees, with the rest paid in food from the family farm. Whittier was a founding member of the American Anti-Slavery Society. His first book of poems was published in 1831.

Whittier's poem 'Barbara Frietchie' celebrates an incident in 1862 during the American Civil War, when a woman in the town of Frederick, Maryland, waved the Union flag in sight of the Confederate army.

Barbara Frietchie

UP from the meadows rich with corn,
Clear in the cool September morn,

The clustered spires of Frederick stand
Green-walled by the hills of Maryland.

Round about them orchards sweep,
Apple- and peach-tree fruited deep,

Fair as a garden of the Lord
To the eyes of the famished rebel horde,

On that pleasant morn of the early fall
When Lee marched over the mountain wall,—

Over the mountains winding down,
Horse and foot, into Frederick town.

Forty flags with their silver stars,
Forty flags with their crimson bars,

Flapped in the morning wind: the sun
Of noon looked down, and saw not one.

Up rose old Barbara Frietchie then,
Bowed with her fourscore years and ten;

Bravest of all in Frederick town,
She took up the flag the men hauled down;

In her attic window the staff she set,
To show that one heart was loyal yet.

Up the street came the rebel tread,
Stonewall Jackson riding ahead.

Under his slouched hat left and right
He glanced: the old flag met his sight.

"Halt!"—the dust-brown ranks stood fast.
"Fire!"—out blazed the rifle-blast.

It shivered the window, pane and sash;
It rent the banner with seam and gash.

Quick, as it fell, from the broken staff
Dame Barbara snatched the silken scarf;

She leaned far out on the window-sill,
And shook it forth with a royal will.

"Shoot, if you must, this old gray head,
But spare your country's flag," she said.

A shade of sadness, a blush of shame,
Over the face of the leader came;

The nobler nature within him stirred
To life at that woman's deed and word:

"Who touches a hair of yon gray head
Dies like a dog! March on!" he said.

All day long through Frederick street
Sounded the tread of marching feet:

All day long that free flag tost
Over the heads of the rebel host.

Ever its torn folds rose and fell
On the loyal winds that loved it well;

And through the hill-gaps, sunset light
Shone over it with a warm good-night.

Barbara Frietchie's work is o'er,
And the Rebel rides on his raids no more.

Honor to her! and let a tear
Fall, for her sake, on Stonewall's bier.

Over Barbara Frietchie's grave
Flag of Freedom and Union, wave!

Peace and order and beauty draw
Round thy symbol of light and law;

And ever the stars above look down
On thy stars below in Frederick town!

John Greenleaf Whittier, 1807-92

Frances Anne Kemble, 1809-93

Fanny Kemble was born in London, the daughter of a well-known family of stage actors. Her mother returned to the stage when Kemble was 10 years old. At the age of 20, Kemble became a highly successful actress. She toured America with her father, where she met and married a rich plantation owner. However, Kemble and her husband argued—partly over the treatment of slaves on her husband's plantations. In 1877, Kemble returned to England, where she died in 1893. Kemble's first book of poems was published in 1844, and she also wrote several plays and journals.

HMS Birkenhead was carrying more than 600 passengers, mainly soldiers, when she struck a hidden rock in 1852. Unable to reach the lifeboats without endangering those who were already aboard, the soldiers stayed on the deck as the ship sank. Kemble's poem 'The Wreck of the Birkenhead' is written in the voice of one of the survivors.

The Wreck of the Birkenhead
A BRITISH TRANSPORT VESSEL LOST ON THE COAST OF AFRICA.
A BALLAD.

AS well as I am able, I'll relate how it befell,
And I trust, sirs, you'll excuse me, if I do not speak it well.
I've lived a hard and wandering life, serving our gracious Queen,
And have nigh forgot my schooling since a soldier I have been.

But however in my untaught speech the tale I tell may thrive,
I shall see the scene before me, to the latest day I live;
And sometimes I have scarce the heart to thank God for saving me,
When I think of my poor comrades, who went down in that dreadful sea,
And my brother's drowning eyes and voice, as a monstrous swirling wave
Rolled him right across my arms, 'twas his winding sheet and grave—

God forgive me! but I wish he had been saved instead of me,
He was a better, braver man than ever I shall be.

The night was still and silent, and the stars shone overhead,
And all were sleeping in the ship, who in one hour were dead.
A heavy swell was rolling in upon the treacherous shore,
And the steersman steered off from the coast, four miles, and barely four.
Six hundred sleeping souls relied upon that helmsman's care,
Poor wretch! the sea has saved him from a terrible despair!
For in that still and starlight night, on that smooth and silent sea,
He sent four hundred sleeping men straight to eternity;
He drove the ship upon the rocks that stretch the waves beneath,
It has been called Point Danger—it should be the Reef of Death.

I was dreaming of old Scotland, the home of my boyish years,
And the sound of the village bagpipe was droning in my ears;
And across the purple heath, behind a screen of fir and oak,
I saw from our low chimney curl the silver blue peat smoke;

My foot was on the door-stone, and my hand was on the lock,
And I heard my mother's voice within—when, suddenly, a shock
Went shuddering through the whole ship's frame, and then a grinding sound,
And the cry was heard above, below, 'Back her! she is aground!'
We heard the water rushing, whence or where we did not know,
And every face was darkened with terror and with woe;
But our officers did all that brave gentlemen could do,
And the sailors did their duty,—they were a gallant crew!
And we poor soldiers, too, sirs, I dare think, did all we could,
We had thought to die upon dry land, not choke in the weltering flood,
But steady, as if we had been on our old parading ground,
We stood till she went to pieces,—and the most of us were drowned.
With the first shock the word was given to put the engine back,
For we saw, when the sea was sucked away, where the reef lay, bare and black,
Right underneath the poor ship's prow, huge, hard, and without motion,
Beneath the sweltering, seething surf, of the restless, rolling ocean;

And it was terrible to hear the engine heave and throb,
Like the huge heart of a giant, with a sound like a heavy sob;
And it cast its shining arms aloft, and the wheels began to turn,
And the mad waves flashed, and whirled, and hissed,
as they felt the strong ship spurn.
Another stroke, and we were off—but the black reef's stony teeth,
Had bitten through her iron ribs, and the sea rushed in beneath,

And up and up the water rose, fast, faster yet and higher,
And leapt into our ship's warm heart, and danced above the fire,
The shining arms fell motionless, and stopped the mighty breath,
And the mad waves sucked us back again, into the jaws of death.

Like horses plunging on the reef, we could see them through the dark,
The flying of their wild white manes made a long and shining mark,
And beyond where the rolling blackness, ridge upon ridge was tost,
Not four miles off, how near, and yet how distant! was the coast.
And now there came another shock, with a hideous crashing sound,
The ship broke right in half—and whirling madly round and round,

Half was sucked down before our eyes, and the water far and near,
Was strewed with hapless, helpless men, whose cries of pain and fear
Drove us wild with terror and with grief, as we stood upon the wreck,
The shivering, shattered, slippery planks, of that miserable deck.

Our wives and children in the boats had been lowered from the side,
And through the dark we heard them, as their wild farewells they cried;
And many a brave man's heart grew sick, as silently he stood,
And heard those bitter wailings rise and sink with the heaving flood:
But not one foot was stirred, and not one hand was raised to fly,
We were bid to stand there on that deck—and we stood still there to die.

At length word of command was given: 'Save yourselves all who can,'
And then, and not till then, away broke every boy and man,
When a loud voice, like an angel's, rose above the infernal din,
'Don't swamp your wives and children, hold back, if you are men!'

We looked into each other's eyes—the boats put off to shore—
And suddenly above my head I felt the billows pour.

I threw my arms abroad to swim—and found that they were cast
(Lord what a gripe I closed them with!) around our gallant mast:
As up the blessed shaft I clomb, shouting in frenzied glee,
The mad waves' thundering voices seemed to call alone for me;
But along the high main-topsail yard I climbed, and crawled, and clung,
And out into the empty night, over the sea I swung;
And others followed in the dark, that fearful, slippery way,
And there we held, and hung, and prayed, for the dear light of day;
And pray you, sirs, that never you may count such hideous hours,
Or know the agony and dread of those speechless prayers of ours.

All in a heap our limbs were twined, holding by one another,
And one man clutched my right arm fast, alas! 'twas not my brother;
I wound my hands around the spar, tight, tight, with the grip of Death,
And in my mortal fear I seized the wood fast in my teeth;

And as each high wave struck the mast, and shook us to and fro,
We could see the sharks' white bellies turn in the sea below.

Just as the day was breaking, I grew dizzy, faint, and sick,
And I heard the man who held me breathing heavily and quick,
His limbs slid slowly down, while with one hand he still did clasp
My arm, and I felt it yielding in the dead man's fatal grasp,
I flung it loose, still holding by one arm alone, while he,
With a heavy plunge fell fathoms down, into the churning sea—
He was dead, sirs, he was dead, yet my eyes grew glazed and dim
With horror, for I felt as if I just had murdered him,
And with that thought my wits gave way, for 'twas followed by another,
At which I shrieked aloud—that I had cast away my brother.

And this is all that I can tell—for I saw and heard no more
Till life came into me again, as I lay upon the shore;
I and a few poor fellows that a boat had fetched away,
By God's grace, from that direful mast, with the blessed light of day.
Our eyes were full of tears, as we looked towards the fatal reef,
Where above the surf the swinging yard seemed to beckon for relief,

For our comrades who lay rolling all round the sunken mast,—
They were brave fellows, sirs, and did their duty to the last:
And I hope that I may say it without unbecoming pride,
There are gallant soldiers, well I know, in many a land beside,
But I think that none but Englishmen like those men would have died.

Frances Anne Kemble, 1809-93

Alfred, Lord Tennyson, 1809-92

Alfred Tennyson was born in Somersby, Lincolnshire, where his father was a clergyman. He went to school in nearby Louth and studied at Cambridge University. His first book of poems Poems by Two Brothers *contained poems by Alfred and his elder brother Charles and was published in 1827, when Alfred was still just 17 years old. Three years later he published the first collection containing only his own poems. Tennyson achieved fame and popularity as a poet—he was appointed Poet Laureate in 1850, and was made a baron in 1883.*

Tennyson's poem 'The Charge of the Light Brigade' relates to an action at the Battle of Balaclava in 1854 during the Crimean War when, because of a muddled order, the British light cavalry made a direct frontal assault on the Russian artillery.

His poem 'The Revenge: A Ballad of the Fleet' tells the story of the last fight of the Elizabethan sailor Sir Richard Grenville and his ship Revenge at the Battle of Flores in 1591.

The Charge of the Light Brigade

HALF a league, half a league,
　　Half a league onward,
All in the valley of Death
　　Rode the six hundred.
"Forward, the Light Brigade!
Charge for the guns!" he said:
Into the valley of Death
Rode the six hundred.

"Forward, the Light Brigade!"
Was there a man dismay'd?
Not tho' the soldier knew
　　Someone had blunder'd:
Theirs not to make reply,
Theirs not to reason why,
Theirs but to do and die:
Into the valley of Death
　　Rode the six hundred.

Cannon to right of them,
Cannon to left of them,
Cannon in front of them
　　Volley'd and thunder'd;
Storm'd at with shot and shell,
Boldly they rode and well,
Into the jaws of Death,
Into the mouth of Hell
　　Rode the six hundred.

Flash'd all their sabres bare,
Flash'd as they turn'd in air
Sabring the gunners there,
Charging an army, while
   All the world wonder'd:
Plunged in the battery-smoke
Right thro' the line they broke;
Cossack and Russian
Reel'd from the sabre-stroke
   Shatter'd and sunder'd.
Then they rode back, but not
   Not the six hundred.

Cannon to right of them,
Cannon to left of them,
Cannon behind them
   Volley'd and thunder'd;
Storm'd at with shot and shell,
While horse and hero fell,
They that had fought so well
Came thro' the jaws of Death,
Back from the mouth of Hell,
All that was left of them,
   Left of six hundred.

When can their glory fade?
O the wild charge they made!
   All the world wonder'd.
Honour the charge they made!
Honour the Light Brigade,
   Noble six hundred!

Alfred, Lord Tennyson, 1809-92

The *Revenge*
A Ballad of the Fleet

I
AT Flores, in the Azores Sir Richard Grenville lay,
And a pinnace, like a flutter'd bird, came flying from far away;
"Spanish ships of war at sea! we have sighted fifty-three!"
Then sware Lord Thomas Howard: "'Fore God I am no coward;
But I cannot meet them here, for my ships are out of gear,
And the half my men are sick. I must fly, but follow quick.
We are six ships of the line; can we fight with fifty-three?"

II
Then spake Sir Richard Grenville: "I know you are no coward;
You fly them for a moment to fight with them again.
But I've ninety men and more that are lying sick ashore.
I should count myself the coward if I left them, my Lord Howard,
To these Inquisition dogs and the devildoms of Spain."

III
So Lord Howard passed away with five ships of war that day,
Till he melted like a cloud in the silent summer heaven;
But Sir Richard bore in hand all his sick men from the land
Very carefully and slow,
Men of Bideford in Devon,
And we laid them on the ballast down below:
For we brought them all aboard,
And they blest him in their pain, that they were not left to Spain,
To the thumb-screw and the stake, for the glory of the Lord.

IV

He had only a hundred seamen to work the ship and to fight,
And he sailed away from Flores till the Spaniard came in sight,
With his huge sea-castles heaving upon the weather bow.
"Shall we fight or shall we fly?
Good Sir Richard, tell us now,
For to fight is but to die!
There'll be little of us left by the time this sun be set."
And Sir Richard said again: "We be all good Englishmen.
Let us bang these dogs of Seville, the children of the devil,
For I never turn'd my back upon Don or devil yet."

V

Sir Richard spoke and he laugh'd, and we roar'd a hurrah and so
The little *Revenge* ran on sheer into the heart of the foe,
With her hundred fighters on deck, and her ninety sick below;
For half of their fleet to the right and half to the left were seen,
And the little *Revenge* ran on thro' the long sea-lane between.

VI

Thousands of their soldiers look'd down from their decks and laugh'd,
Thousands of their seamen made mock at the mad little craft
Running on and on, till delay'd
By their mountain-like San Philip that, of fifteen hundred tons,
And up-shadowing high above us with her yawning tiers of guns,
Took the breath from our sails, and we stay'd.

VII

And while now the great San Philip hung above us like a cloud
Whence the thunderbolt will fall
Long and loud,

Four galleons drew away
From the Spanish fleet that day.
And two upon the larboard and two upon the starboard lay,
And the battle-thunder broke from them all.

    VIII
But anon the great San Philip, she bethought herself and went,
Having that within her womb that had left her ill content;
And the rest they came aboard us, and they fought us hand to hand,
For a dozen times they came with their pikes and musqueteers,
And a dozen times we shook 'em off as a dog that shakes his ears
When he leaps from the water to the land.

    IX
And the sun went down, and the stars came out far over the summer sea,
But never a moment ceased the fight of the one and the fifty-three.
Ship after ship, the whole night long, their high-built galleons came,
Ship after ship, the whole night long, with her battle-thunder and flame;
Ship after ship, the whole night long, drew back with her dead and her shame.
For some were sunk and many were shatter'd and so could fight us no more—
God of battles, was ever a battle like this in the world before?

    X
For he said, "Fight on! fight on!"
Tho' his vessel was all but a wreck;
And it chanced that, when half of the short summer night was gone,
With a grisly wound to be drest he had left the deck,
But a bullet struck him that was dressing it suddenly dead,
And himself he was wounded again in the side and the head,
And he said, "Fight on! fight on!"

XI

And the night went down, and the sun smiled out far over the summer sea,
And the Spanish fleet with broken sides lay round us all in a ring;
But they dared not touch us again, for they fear'd that we still could sting,
So they watch'd what the end would be.
And we had not fought them in vain,
But in perilous plight were we,
Seeing forty of our poor hundred were slain,
And half of the rest of us maim'd for life
In the crash of the cannonades and the desperate strife;
And the sick men down in the hold were most of them stark and cold,
And the pikes were all broken or bent, and the powder was all of it spent;
And the masts and the rigging were lying over the side;
But Sir Richard cried in his English pride:
"We have fought such a fight for a day and a night
As may never be fought again!
We have won great glory, my men!
And a day less or more
At sea or ashore,
We die—does it matter when?
Sink me the ship, Master Gunner—sink her, split her in twain!
Fall into the hands of God, not into the hands of Spain!"

XII

And the gunner said, "Ay, ay," but the seamen made reply:
"We have children, we have wives,
And the Lord hath spared our lives.
We will make the Spaniard promise, if we yield, to let us go;
We shall live to fight again and to strike another blow."
And the lion there lay dying, and they yielded to the foe.

XIII

And the stately Spanish men to their flagship bore him then,
Where they laid him by the mast, old Sir Richard caught at last,
And they praised him to his face with their courtly foreign grace;
But he rose upon their decks, and he cried:
"I have fought for Queen and Faith like a valiant man and true;
I have only done my duty as a man is bound to do.
With a joyful spirit I Sir Richard Grenville die!"
And he fell upon their decks, and he died.

XIV

And they stared at the dead that had been so valiant and true,
And had holden the power and glory of Spain so cheap
That he dared her with one little ship and his English few;
Was he devil or man? He was devil for aught they knew,
But they sank his body with honour down into the deep.
And they mann'd the *Revenge* with a swarthier alien crew,
And away she sail'd with her loss and long'd for her own;
When a wind from the lands they had ruin'd awoke from sleep,
And the water began to heave and the weather to moan,
And or ever that evening ended a great gale blew,
And a wave like the wave that is raised by an earthquake grew,
Till it smote on their hulls and their sails and their masts and their flags,
And the whole sea plunged and fell on the shot-shatter'd navy of Spain,
And the little *Revenge* herself went down by the island crags
To be lost evermore in the main.

Alfred, Lord Tennyson, 1809-92

Robert Browning, 1812–89

Robert Browning was born in Walworth, Surrey (now part of south London). His father worked for the Bank of England and collected an impressive library of 6,000 books. Browning was taught at home by a private tutor; he was unable to go to university which was only open to members of the Church of England. However, by the age of fourteen he was already fluent in French, Greek, Italian and Latin. His first book of poetry was published in 1833.

Browning's poem 'An Incident of the French Camp' retells a story from the Napoleonic Wars, when Napoleon's forces were briefly halted by the Austrian army at the city of Ratisbon (now Regensburg) in April 1809.

An Incident of the French Camp

YOU know, we French storm'd Ratisbon:
    A mile or so away
On a little mound, Napoleon
    Stood on our storming-day;
With neck out-thrust, you fancy how,
    Legs wide, arms lock'd behind,
As if to balance the prone brow
    Oppressive with its mind.

Just as perhaps he mus'd "My plans
    That soar, to earth may fall,
Let once my army leader Lannes
    Waver at yonder wall,"—
Out 'twixt the battery smokes there flew
    A rider, bound on bound
Full-galloping; nor bridle drew
    Until he reach'd the mound.

Then off there flung in smiling joy,
    And held himself erect
By just his horse's mane, a boy:
    You hardly could suspect—
(So tight he kept his lips compress'd,
    Scarce any blood came through)
You look'd twice ere you saw his breast
    Was all but shot in two.

"Well," cried he, "Emperor, by God's grace
    We've got you Ratisbon!
The Marshal's in the market-place,
    And you'll be there anon
To see your flag-bird flap his vans
    Where I, to heart's desire,
Perch'd him!" The chief's eye flash'd; his plans
    Soar'd up again like fire,

The chief's eye flash'd; but presently
    Soften'd itself, as sheathes
A film the mother-eagle's eye
    When her bruis'd eaglet breathes.
"You're wounded!" "Nay," the soldier's pride
    Touch'd to the quick, he said:
"I'm kill'd, Sire!" And his chief beside,
    Smiling the boy fell dead.

Robert Browning, 1812–89

Robert Traill Spence Lowell, 1816-91

Robert Traill Spence Lowell was born in Boston, Massachusetts, the son of a Unitarian minister. He went to school in Northampton, Massachusetts, and studied at Harvard University and Harvard Medical School. After completing his medical studies, Lowell became a clergyman in the Episcopal Church. His first novel was published in 1858 and his first book of poems in 1860.

Lowell's poem 'The Relief of Lucknow' describes the arrival of Sir Colin Campbell's troops at the Indian city of Lucknow in 1857. Along with large parts of India, Lucknow belonged to the British East India Company but, after a period of misrule, Indian soldiers rebelled against their British rulers. The rebellion itself may have been justified, but the rebels vented their anger in killing 200 women and children at Cawnpore (now Kanpur) and the British under siege at Lucknow feared a similar fate. The Siege of Lucknow began in June 1857. In September a first attempt to free the inhabitants failed, and it was not until November that the the siege was finally lifted.

The Relief of Lucknow

OH, that last day in Lucknow fort!
    We knew that it was the last;
That the enemy's lines crept surely on,
    And the end was coming fast.

To yield to that foe meant worse than death;
    And the men and we all worked on;
It was one day more of smoke and roar,
    And then it would all be done.

There was one of us, a corporal's wife,
    A fair, young, gentle thing,
Wasted with fever in the siege,
    And her mind was wandering.

She lay on the ground, in her Scottish plaid,
    And I took her head on my knee;
"When my father comes hame frae the pleugh," she said,
    "Oh, then please waken me."

She slept like a child on her father's floor,
    In the flecking of woodbine shade,
When the house-dog sprawls by the open door,
    And the mother's wheel is stayed.

It was smoke and roar and powder-stench,
    And hopeless waiting for death;
And the soldier's wife, like a full-tired child,
    Seemed scarce to draw her breath.

I sank to sleep, and I had my dream
    Of an English village-lane,
And wall and garden;—but one wild scream
    Brought me back to the roar again.

There Jessie Brown stood listening
    Till a sudden gladness broke
All over her face; and she caught my hand
    And drew me near as she spoke:—

"The Hielanders! Oh, dinna ye hear
    The slogan far awa'
The McGregor's. Oh! I ken it weel
    It's the grandest o' them a'!

"God bless the bonny Hielanders!
    We're saved! we're saved!" she cried;
And fell on her knees; and thanks to God
    Flowed forth like a full flood-tide.

Along the battery line her cry
    Had fallen among the men,
And they started back;—they were there to die;
    But was life so near them, then?

They listened for life; the rattling fire
    Far off, and the far-off roar,
Were all, and the colonel shook his head,
    And they turned to their guns once more.

But Jessie said, "The slogan's done;
    But winna ye hear it noo?
'The Campbells are coming'? It's no a dream;
    Our succors hae broken through!"

We heard the roar and the rattle afar,
    But the pipes we could not hear;
So the men plied their work of hopeless war,
    And knew that the end was near.

It was not long ere it made its way,
    A thrilling, ceaseless sound:
It was no noise from the strife afar,
    Or the sappers under ground.

It was the pipes of the Highlanders!
    And now they played "Auld Lang Syne."
It came to our men like the voice of God,
    And they shouted along the line.

And they wept, and shook one another's hands,
    And the women sobbed in a crowd;
And every one knelt down where he stood,
    And we all thanked God aloud.

That happy time, when we welcomed them,
    Our men put Jessie first;
And the general gave her his hand, and cheers
    Like a storm from the soldiers burst.

And the pipers' ribbons and tartan streamed,
    Marching round and round our line;
And our joyful cheers were broken with tears,
    As the pipes played "Auld Lang Syne."

Robert Traill Spence Lowell, 1816-91

Arthur Hugh Clough, 1819-61

Arthur Hugh Clough was born in Liverpool, the son of a cotton merchant. In 1822 the family moved to America but, at the age of 9, Clough was sent to school in England, first at Chester and then Rugby. He went to university in Oxford, where he later became a tutor. As well as his academic work, Clough also worked as an unpaid secretary for his wife's cousin Florence Nightingale. He published his first book of poetry in 1848.

Clough's poem 'Say not the Struggle Naught Availeth' was published in 1849 at a time when many of the causes he believed in seemed to be foundering. It's underlying message, 'Don't give up,' has seldom been more eloquently expressed.

Say not the Struggle Nought Availeth

SAY not the struggle nought availeth,
   The labour and the wounds are vain,
The enemy faints not, nor faileth,
   And as things have been they remain.

If hopes were dupes, fears may be liars;
   It may be, in yon smoke concealed,
Your comrades chase e'en now the fliers,
   And, but for you, possess the field.

For while the tired waves, vainly breaking
   Seem here no painful inch to gain,
Far back through creeks and inlets making,
   Comes silent, flooding in, the main.

And not by eastern windows only,
   When daylight comes, comes in the light,
In front the sun climbs slow, how slowly,
   But westward, look, the land is bright.

Arthur Hugh Clough, 1819-61

Charles Kingsley, 1819-75

Charles Kingsley was born in Devon, where his father was a clergyman. He went to school in Helston and Bristol, and then to university in London and Cambridge. Kingsley became a minister in the Church of England and Professor of History at Cambridge University. He was also chaplain to Queen Victoria and tutor to the Prince of Wales. As a churchman Kingsley rose to the rank of canon, first at Chester Cathedral and later at Westminster Abbey. His first novel was published in 1848 and his first book of poems in 1858.

The poem 'Young and Old' appeared in his most famous novel The Water Babies in 1863.

Young and Old

WHEN all the world is young, lad,
    And all the trees are green;
And every goose a swan, lad,
    And every lass a queen;
Then hey for boot and horse, lad,
    And round the world away;
Young blood must have its course, lad,
    And every dog his day.

When all the world is old, lad,
    And all the trees are brown;
And all the sport is stale, lad,
    And all the wheels run down;
Creep home, and take your place there,
    The spent and maimed among:
God grant you find one face there,
    You loved when all was young.

Charles Kingsley, 1819-75

Herman Melville, 1819-91

Herman Melville was born in New York. His father died when he was 13. After a series of jobs, Melville became a sailor in 1829 but a few years later, he jumped ship in the Marquesas Islands and spent a month living among the Polynesian islanders. Melville's first successful books were based on his experiences among the islanders. His first book of poetry was a collection of poems about the American Civil War and was published in 1866 when Melville was 47 years old. Today, Melville's most famous work is the novel Moby Dick.

The Battle of Malvern Hill marked the end of the Seven Days' Battles, when Confederate troops under General Lee had forced the Union Army of the Potomac into a week-long retreat. At Malvern Hill, General McClellan found a strong position and successfully turned the fight against Lee.

Malvern Hill
(July, 1862.)

YE elms that wave on Malvern Hill
    In prime of morn and May,
Recall ye how McClellan's men
    Here stood at bay?
While deep within yon forest dim
    Our rigid comrades lay—
Some with the cartridge in their mouth,
Others with fixed arms lifted South—
    Invoking so
The cypress glades? Ah wilds of woe!

The spires of Richmond, late beheld
    Through rifts in musket-haze,
Were closed from view in clouds of dust
    On leaf-walled ways,
Where streamed our wagons in caravan;
    And the Seven Nights and Days
Of march and fast, retreat and fight,
Pinched our grimed faces to ghastly plight—
    Does the elm wood
Recall the haggard beards of blood?

The battle-smoked flag, with stars eclipsed,
    We followed (it never fell!)—
In silence husbanded our strength—
    Received their yell;
Till on this slope we patient turned
    With cannon ordered well;
Reverse we proved was not defeat;
But ah, the sod what thousands meet!—
    Does Malvern Wood
Bethink itself, and muse and brood?

    We elms of Malvern Hill
    Remember every thing;
    But sap the twig will fill:
    Wag the world how it will,
    Leaves must be green in Spring.

Herman Melville, 1819-91

Christina Rossetti, 1830-94

Christina Rossetti was born in London's West End. Her father was the Italian poet Gabriele Rossetti who had come to London as an exile. Christina Rossetti left school at 14, but continued to follow her interest in writing and poetry. Christina's brothers and sister also became writers, and her older brother Dante Gabriel Rossetti achieved fame as an artist and poet. Christina Rossetti's first poems appeared in print when she was just 18, and she published her first book of poems in 1862. She died at home in Bloomsbury at the age of 64.

Rossetti's poem 'Remember' asks friends who will live on after her death to allow their lives to move on without her.

Remember

REMEMBER me when I am gone away,
   Gone far away into the silent land;
   When you can no more hold me by the hand,
Nor I half turn to go yet turning stay.
Remember me when no more day by day
   You tell me of our future that you plann'd:
   Only remember me; you understand
It will be late to counsel then or pray.
Yet if you should forget me for a while
   And afterwards remember, do not grieve:
   For if the darkness and corruption leave
   A vestige of the thoughts that once I had,
Better by far you should forget and smile
   Than that you should remember and be sad.

Christina Rossetti, 1830-94

Thomas Hardy, 1840 – 1928

Hardy was born in Upper Bockhampton, Dorset, where his father was a stonemason and builder. His mother taught him at home until the age of 8, when he went to school in Dorchester. At the age of 16, he was apprenticed to an architect, and went on to study architecture at London University before moving back to Dorset. Hardy published his first novel in 1871 and he continued to write and publish novels until 1897. His first book of poems was published in 1898, and contained poems written over the previous thirty years.

The two poems published here are from his later work and both were written during the First World War. Both poems speak of what will endure in times of great upheaval and loss.

Heredity

I AM the family face;
Flesh perishes, I live on,
Projecting trait and trace
Through time to times anon,
And leaping from place to place
Over oblivion.

The years-heired feature that can
In curve and voice and eye
Despise the human span
Of durance—that is I;
The eternal thing in man,
That heeds no call to die

Thomas Hardy, 1840 – 1928

In Time of 'The Breaking of Nations'

ONLY a man harrowing clods
   In a slow silent walk
With an old horse that stumbles and nods
   Half asleep as they stalk.

Only thin smoke without flame
   From the heaps of couch-grass;
Yet this will go onward the same
   Though Dynasties pass.

Yonder a maid and her wight
   Come whispering by:
War's annals will cloud into night
   Ere their story die.

Thomas Hardy, 1840 - 1928

Gerard Manley Hopkins, 1844-89

Gerard Manley Hopkins was born in Stratford, Essex. His father, Manley Hopkins, was a published poet and literary critic. The family moved to Hampstead when Hopkins was 8, and he went to Highgate School and then to Oxford University. Hopkins converted to Catholicism and joined the Jesuit priesthood. Most of his poems were not published until after his death.

The poem 'Inversnaid' is among his best-loved poems. Inversnaid on Loch Lomond was a popular destination for Victorian tourists because of its association with the outlaw Rob Roy MacGregor.

As a priest, Hopkins' duties included visiting the sick. The poem 'Felix Randal' tells of the death of one of his parishioners, and remembers the dead man as he appeared in his prime.

Inversnaid

THIS darksome burn, horseback brown,
His rollrock highroad roaring down,
In coop and in comb the fleece of his foam
Flutes and low to the lake falls home.

A windpuff-bonnet of fawn-froth
Turns and twindles over the broth
Of a pool so pitchblack, fell-frowning,
It rounds and rounds Despair to drowning.

Degged with dew, dappled with dew
Are the groins of the braes that the brook treads through,
Wiry heathpacks, flitches of fern,
And the beadbonny ash that sits over the burn.

What would the world be, once bereft
Of wet and of wildness? Let them be left,
O let them be left, wildness and wet;
Long live the weeds and the wilderness yet.

Gerard Manley Hopkins, 1844–89

Felix Randal

FELIX RANDAL the farrier, O he is dead then? my duty all ended,
Who have watched his mould of man, big-boned and hardy-handsome
Pining, pining, till time when reason rambled in it and some
Fatal four disorders, fleshed there, all contended?

Sickness broke him. Impatient he cursed at first, but mended
Being anointed and all; though a heavenlier heart began some
Months earlier, since I had our sweet reprieve and ransom
Tendered to him. Ah well, God rest him all road ever he offended!

This seeing the sick endears them to us, us too it endears.
My tongue had taught thee comfort, touch had quenched thy tears,
Thy tears that touched my heart, child, Felix, poor Felix Randal;

How far from then forethought of, all thy more boisterous years,
When thou at the random grim forge, powerful amidst peers,
Didst fettle for the great grey drayhorse his bright and battering sandal!

Gerard Manley Hopkins, 1844-89

Thomas Armstrong, 1848 – 1919

Tommy Armstrong was born in Shotley Bridge, Co. Durham. He grew up in a coal mining community and he too became a miner or pitman, but he also composed poems and songs, which he had printed to sell in local pubs. Conditions in the coal pits were dangerous and, in 1882, seventy four miners were killed in an explosion at Trimdon Grange Colliery. Armstong wrote 'The Trimdon Grange Explosion' to help raise money for the families of the dead miners. Many of Armstrong's verses were in the miners' dialect of Pitmatic, but for this commemorative piece he chose to write in standard English.

The Trimdon Grange Explosion

LET'S not think of tomorrow,
Lest we disappointed be;
Our joys may turn to sorrow,
As we all may daily see.
Today we're strong and healthy,
But how soon there comes a change.
As we may see from the explosion
That has been at Trimdon Grange.

Men and boys left home that morning
For to earn their daily bread,
Little thought before the evening
They'd be numbered with the dead;
Let us think of Mrs Burnett,
Once had sons and now has none -
With the Trimdon Grange explosion,
Joseph, George and James are gone.

February left behind it
What will never be forgot;
Weeping widows, helpless children
May be found in many a cot.
Little children kind and loving
From their homes each day would run;
For to meet their father's coming
As each hard day's work was done.

Now they ask if father's left them,
And the mother hangs her head,
With a weeping widow's feelings,
Tells the child its father's dead.
Homes that once were blessed with comfort
Guided by a father's care
Now are solemn, sad and gloomy,
Since the father is not there.

God protect each lonely widow,
Help to raise each drooping head;
Be a Father to the orphans,
Never let them cry for bread.
Death will pay us all a visit;
They have only gone before.
We may meet the Trimdon victims
Where explosions are no more.

Thomas Armstrong, 1848 - 1919

William Ernest Henley, 1849 – 1903

William Ernest Henley was born in Gloucester, where his father was a bookseller. He attended The Crypt School, where he was inspired by the brilliant schoolmaster T. E. Brown. From the age of 12, Henley suffered from tuberculosis of the bone, and his left leg was amputated when he was 18. His first collection of poems was published in 1888. His daughter Margaret, who died at the age of 5, was the inspiration for the character of Wendy in Peter Pan. In 1902, Henley fell from a railway carriage, and the tuberculosis reawakened within him; he died the next year.

Henley's poem 'Invictus' continues to inspire people across the world. The Latin title was given to the poem by Sir Arthur Quiller-Couch and means 'Unconquered.'

Invictus

OUT of the night that covers me,
   Black as the pit from pole to pole,
I thank whatever gods may be
   For my unconquerable soul.

In the fell clutch of circumstance
   I have not winced nor cried aloud.
Under the bludgeonings of chance
   My head is bloody, but unbowed.

Beyond this place of wrath and tears
   Looms but the Horror of the shade,
And yet the menace of the years
   Finds and shall find me unafraid.

It matters not how strait the gate,
   How charged with punishments the scroll,
I am the master of my fate,
   I am the captain of my soul.

William Ernest Henley, 1849 – 1903

Robert Louis Stevenson, 1850-94

Robert Louis Stevenson was born in Edinburgh, the son of a lighthouse engineer. He was a sickly child with a tendency to coughs and fevers, and he found it hard to fit in at school. He went to Edinburgh University and qualified as an advocate but never practised law, instead becoming famous as a writer. He travelled first in Europe and then America, but his poor health meant that on more than one occasion he nearly died. He eventually settled with his wife in Samoa, where he took the Samoan name 'Tusitala,' meaning Storyteller.

The deceptively simple poem 'Where Go The Boats?' was published in Stevenson's book of poetry about childhood, A Child's Garden of Verses.

'Ticonderoga' retells a Highland legend, although the central character should correctly be given as Major Duncan Campbell of Inverawe who died in the assault on Fort Ticonderoga (then Fort Carillon) in 1758—Stevenson acknowledged this in his own notes to the poem.

Where Go the Boats?

DARK brown is the river.
Golden is the sand.
It flows along for ever,
With trees on either hand.

Green leaves a-floating,
Castles of the foam,
Boats of mine a-boating—
Where will all come home?

On goes the river
And out past the mill,
Away down the valley,
Away down the hill.

Away down the river,
A hundred miles or more,
Other little children
Shall bring my boats ashore.

Robert Louis Stevenson, 1850–94

Ticonderoga, a Legend of the West Highlands

THIS is the tale of the man
Who heard a word in the night
In the land of the heathery hills,
In the days of the feud and the fight.
By the sides of the rainy sea,
Where never a stranger came,
On the awful lips of the dead,
He heard the outlandish name.
It sang in his sleeping ears,
It hummed in his waking head:
The name—Ticonderoga,
The utterance of the dead.

I. The Saying of the Name

ON the loch-sides of Appin,
When the mist blew from the sea,
A Stewart stood with a Cameron:
An angry man was he.
The blood beat in his ears,
The blood ran hot to his head,
The mist blew from the sea,
And there was the Cameron dead.
'O, what have I done to my friend,
O, what have I done to mysel',
That he should be cold and dead,
And I in the danger of all?

Nothing but danger about me,
Danger behind and before,
Death at wait in the heather
In Appin and Mamore,
Hate at all of the ferries
And death at each of the fords,
Camerons priming gunlocks
And Camerons sharpening swords.'

But this was a man of counsel,
This was a man of a score,
There dwelt no pawkier Stewart
In Appin or Mamore.
He looked on the blowing mist,
He looked on the awful dead,
And there came a smile on his face
And there slipped a thought in his head.

Out over cairn and moss,
Out over scrog and scaur,
He ran as runs the clansman
That bears the cross of war.
His heart beat in his body,
His hair clove to his face,
When he came at last in the gloaming
To the dead man's brother's place.
The east was white with the moon,
The west with the sun was red,
And there, in the house-doorway,
Stood the brother of the dead.

'I have slain a man to my danger,
I have slain a man to my death.
I put my soul in your hands,'
The panting Stewart saith.
'I lay it bare in your hands,
For I know your hands are leal;
And be you my targe and bulwark
From the bullet and the steel.'

Then up and spoke the Cameron,
And gave him his hand again:
'There shall never a man in Scotland
Set faith in me in vain;
And whatever man you have slaughtered,
Of whatever name or line,
By my sword and yonder mountain,
I make your quarrel mine.
I bid you in to my fireside,
I share with you house and hall;
It stands upon my honour
To see you safe from all.'

It fell in the time of midnight,
When the fox barked in the den
And the plaids were over the faces
In all the houses of men,
That as the living Cameron
Lay sleepless on his bed,
Out of the night and the other world,
Came in to him the dead.

'My blood is on the heather,
My bones are on the hill;
There is joy in the home of ravens
That the young shall eat their fill.
My blood is poured in the dust,
My soul is spilled in the air;
And the man that has undone me
Sleeps in my brother's care.'

'I'm wae for your death, my brother,
But if all of my house were dead,
I couldnae withdraw the plighted hand,
Nor break the word once said.'

'O, what shall I say to our father,
In the place to which I fare?
O, what shall I say to our mother,
Who greets to see me there?
And to all the kindly Camerons
That have lived and died long-syne—
Is this the word you send them,
Fause-hearted brother mine?'

'It's neither fear nor duty,
It's neither quick nor dead
Shall gar me withdraw the plighted hand,
Or break the word once said.'

Thrice in the time of midnight,
When the fox barked in the den,
And the plaids were over the faces
In all the houses of men,

Thrice as the living Cameron
Lay sleepless on his bed,
Out of the night and the other world
Came in to him the dead,
And cried to him for vengeance
On the man that laid him low;
And thrice the living Cameron
Told the dead Cameron, no.

'Thrice have you seen me, brother,
But now shall see me no more,
Till you meet your angry fathers
Upon the farther shore.
Thrice have I spoken, and now,
Before the cock be heard,
I take my leave for ever
With the naming of a word.
It shall sing in your sleeping ears,
It shall hum in your waking head,
The name—Ticonderoga,
And the warning of the dead.'

Now when the night was over
And the time of people's fears,
The Cameron walked abroad,
And the word was in his ears.
'Many a name I know,
But never a name like this;
O, where shall I find a skilly man
Shall tell me what it is?'
With many a man he counselled

Of high and low degree,
With the herdsmen on the mountains
And the fishers of the sea.
And he came and went unweary,
And read the books of yore,
And the runes that were written of old
On stones upon the moor.
And many a name he was told,
But never the name of his fears—
Never, in east or west,
The name that rang in his ears:
Names of men and of clans;
Names for the grass and the tree,
For the smallest tarn in the mountains,
The smallest reef in the sea:
Names for the high and low,
The names of the craig and the flat;
But in all the land of Scotland,
Never a name like that.

II. *The Seeking of the Name*

AND now there was speech in the south,
And a man of the south that was wise,
A periwig'd lord of London,
Called on the clans to rise.
And the riders rode, and the summons
Came to the western shore,
To the land of the sea and the heather,
To Appin and Mamore.

It called on all to gather
From every scrog and scaur,
That loved their fathers' tartan
And the ancient game of war.

And down the watery valley
And up the windy hill,
Once more, as in the olden,
The pipes were sounding shrill;
Again in highland sunshine
The naked steel was bright;
And the lads, once more in tartan
Went forth again to fight.

'O, why should I dwell here
With a weird upon my life,
When the clansmen shout for battle
And the war-swords clash in strife?
I cannae joy at feast,
I cannae sleep in bed,
For the wonder of the word
And the warning of the dead.
It sings in my sleeping ears,
It hums in my waking head,
The name—Ticonderoga,
The utterance of the dead.
Then up, and with the fighting men
To march away from here,
Till the cry of the great war-pipe
Shall drown it in my ear!'

Where flew King George's ensign
The plaided soldiers went:
They drew the sword in Germany,
In Flanders pitched the tent.
The bells of foreign cities
Rang far across the plain:
They passed the happy Rhine,
They drank the rapid Main.
Through Asiatic jungles
The Tartans filed their way,
And the neighing of the war-pipes
Struck terror in Cathay.

'Many a name have I heard,' he thought,
'In all the tongues of men,
Full many a name both here and there.
Full many both now and then.
When I was at home in my father's house
In the land of the naked knee,
Between the eagles that fly in the lift
And the herrings that swim in the sea,
And now that I am a captain-man
With a braw cockade in my hat—
Many a name have I heard,' he thought,
'But never a name like that.'

III. *The Place of the Name*

THERE fell a war in a woody place,
Lay far across the sea,
A war of the march in the mirk midnight

And the shot from behind the tree,
The shaven head and the painted face,
The silent foot in the wood,
In a land of a strange, outlandish tongue
That was hard to be understood.

It fell about the gloaming
The general stood with his staff,
He stood and he looked east and west
With little mind to laugh.
'Far have I been and much have I seen,
And kent both gain and loss,
But here we have woods on every hand
And a kittle water to cross.
Far have I been and much have I seen,
But never the beat of this;
And there's one must go down to that waterside
To see how deep it is.'

It fell in the dusk of the night
When unco things betide,
The skilly captain, the Cameron,
Went down to that waterside.
Canny and soft the captain went;
And a man of the woody land,
With the shaven head and the painted face,
Went down at his right hand.
It fell in the quiet night,
There was never a sound to ken;
But all of the woods to the right and the left
Lay filled with the painted men.

'Far have I been and much have I seen,
Both as a man and boy,
But never have I set forth a foot
On so perilous an employ.'
It fell in the dusk of the night
When unco things betide,
That he was aware of a captain-man
Drew near to the waterside.
He was aware of his coming
Down in the gloaming alone;
And he looked in the face of the man
And lo! the face was his own.
'This is my weird,' he said,
'And now I ken the worst;
For many shall fall the morn,
But I shall fall with the first.
O, you of the outland tongue,
You of the painted face,
This is the place of my death;
Can you tell me the name of the place?'
'Since the Frenchmen have been here
They have called it Sault-Marie;
But that is a name for priests,
And not for you and me.
It went by another word,'
Quoth he of the shaven head:
'It was called Ticonderoga
In the days of the great dead.'

And it fell on the morrow's morning,
In the fiercest of the fight,
That the Cameron bit the dust
As he foretold at night;
And far from the hills of heather
Far from the isles of the sea,
He sleeps in the place of the name
As it was doomed to be.

Robert Louis Stevenson, 1850-94

Sir Henry Newbolt, 1862 - 1938

Henry Newbolt was born in Bilston near Wolverhampton. His father had been vicar at the parish church, but died when Newbolt was not quite four years old. The family then moved to nearby Walsall where Newbolt went to school. He was Head Boy at Caistor College, and went on to Oxford University. In 1887 he began work as a barrister.

Newbolt's best-known poem 'Vitaï Lampada' was inspired by the Battle of Abu Klea in 1885 and tells how, in the heat of battle, a soldier falls back on lessons learned on the school cricket pitch. The title Vitaï Lampada means 'The Torch of Life' and is a quotation from the Roman poet Lucretius.

The poem 'Drake's Drum' recalls the story that in 1596, as Sir Francis Drake lay dying on his ship, he ordered that his drum be returned to his home at Buckland Abbey and that if England were in danger, someone should beat the drum and he would return. The poem is written in imitation of the sounds of Devon speech.

the Close: *the name of the cricket pitch at Clifton College, Bristol.*
a square that broke: *an infantry square was a defensive battle formation.*
Gatling: *an early make of machine gun; the gun which jammed at Abu Klea was in fact a Gardner.*

Vitaï Lampada

THERE'S a breathless hush in the Close to-night—
Ten to make and the match to win—
A bumping pitch and a blinding light,
An hour to play and the last man in.
And it's not for the sake of a ribboned coat,
Or the selfish hope of a season's fame,
But his Captain's hand on his shoulder smote
'Play up! play up! and play the game!'

The sand of the desert is sodden red,—
Red with the wreck of a square that broke;—
The Gatling's jammed and the colonel dead,
And the regiment blind with dust and smoke.
The river of death has brimmed his banks,
And England's far, and Honour a name,
But the voice of a schoolboy rallies the ranks,
'Play up! play up! and play the game!'

This is the word that year by year
While in her place the School is set
Every one of her sons must hear,
And none that hears it dare forget.
This they all with a joyful mind
Bear through life like a torch in flame,
And falling fling to the host behind—
'Play up! play up! and play the game!'

Sir Henry Newbolt, 1862 – 1938

Drake's Drum

DRAKE he's in his hammock an' a thousand mile away,
    (Capten, art tha sleepin' there below?)
Slung atween the round shot in Nombre Dios Bay,
    An' dreamin' arl the time o' Plymouth Hoe.
Yarnder lumes the island, yarnder lie the ships,
    Wi' sailor lads a-dancin' heel-an'-toe,
An' the shore-lights flashin', an' the night-tide dashin'
    He sees et arl so plainly as he saw et long ago.

Drake he was a Devon man, an' ruled the Devon seas,
    (Capten, art tha sleepin' there below?),
Rovin' tho' his death fell, he went wi' heart at ease,
    An' dreamin' arl the time o' Plymouth Hoe,
'Take my drum to England, hang et by the shore,
    Strike et when your powder's runnin' low;
If the Dons sight Devon, I'll quit the port o' Heaven,
    An' drum them up the Channel as we drummed them long ago.'

Drake he's in his hammock till the great Armadas come,
    (Capten, art tha sleepin' there below?),
Slung atween the round shot, listenin' for the drum,
    An' dreamin' arl the time o' Plymouth Hoe.
Call him on the deep sea, call him up the Sound,
    Call him when ye sail to meet the foe;
Where the old trade's plyin' an' the old flag flyin',
    They shall find him, ware an' wakin', as they found him long ago.

Sir Henry Newbolt, 1862 – 1938

Rudyard Kipling, 1865 – 1936

Kipling was born in Bombay (now Mumbai), India, into a well-connected British family. At the age of five, he was sent to foster parents in Southsea, England, where he was very unhappy but remained until his mother's return from India, seven years later. Kipling returned to India at the age of sixteen, but would eventually settle in England after living briefly in America. He published his first book of poems in 1886 and went on to become a celebrated writer. His works for younger children include the Just So Stories and Jungle Book. Kipling turned down a knighthood and the Order of Merit, but accepted the Nobel Prize for Literature in 1907. In 1915, Kipling was devastated by the death of his son in the First World War, and this tragedy seems to have shaped the last twenty years of his life.

Kipling wrote the poem 'If—' for his own son, and it has gone on to inspire generations of boys and men. His poem 'The Way Through The Woods' appeared in the same collection.

If—

IF you can keep your head when all about you
Are losing theirs and blaming it on you,
If you can trust yourself when all men doubt you,
But make allowance for their doubting too;
If you can wait and not be tired by waiting,
Or being lied about, don't deal in lies,
Or being hated, don't give way to hating,
And yet don't look too good, nor talk too wise:

If you can dream—and not make dreams your master;
If you can think—and not make thoughts your aim;
If you can meet with Triumph and Disaster
And treat those two impostors just the same;
If you can bear to hear the truth you've spoken
Twisted by knaves to make a trap for fools,
Or watch the things you gave your life to, broken,
And stoop and build 'em up with worn-out tools:

If you can make one heap of all your winnings
And risk it on one turn of pitch-and-toss,
And lose, and start again at your beginnings
And never breathe a word about your loss;
If you can force your heart and nerve and sinew
To serve your turn long after they are gone,
And so hold on when there is nothing in you
Except the Will which says to them: 'Hold on!'

If you can talk with crowds and keep your virtue,
Or walk with Kings—nor lose the common touch,
If neither foes nor loving friends can hurt you,
If all men count with you, but none too much;
If you can fill the unforgiving minute
With sixty seconds' worth of distance run,
Yours is the Earth and everything that's in it,
And—which is more—you'll be a Man, my son!

Rudyard Kipling, 1865 - 1936

The Way through the Woods

THEY shut the road through the woods
Seventy years ago.
Weather and rain have undone it again,
And now you would never know
There was once a road through the woods
Before they planted the trees.
It is underneath the coppice and heath
And the thin anemones.
Only the keeper sees
That, where the ring-dove broods,
And the badgers roll at ease,
There was once a road through the woods.

Yet, if you enter the woods
Of a summer evening late,
When the night-air cools on the trout-ringed pools
Where the otter whistles his mate,
(They fear not men in the woods,
Because they see so few.)
You will hear the beat of a horse's feet,
And the swish of a skirt in the dew,
Steadily cantering through
The misty solitudes,
As though they perfectly knew
The old lost road through the woods ...
But there is no road through the woods.

Rudyard Kipling, 1865 – 1936

Henry Lawson, 1867 – 1922

Lawson was born in Grenfell, New South Wales, where his Norwegian-born father was a gold miner. His mother was a political activist who later followed her son as a poet. While still at school, Lawson suffered an ear infection and by the age of 14, he was completely deaf. On leaving school, Lawson worked as builder and housepainter, but always found time for his writing. His first collection was a mix of poetry and prose. He published many books and won respect as a writer, but his personal life was always troubled. Although he died in relative poverty, he was awarded a State Funeral.

Like all his work, Lawson's poem 'The Glass on the Bar' is set in the Australia he knew so well.

The Glass on the Bar

THREE bushmen one morning rode up to an inn,
And one of them called for the drinks with a grin;
They'd only returned from a trip to the North,
And, eager to greet them, the landlord came forth.
He absently poured out a glass of Three Star,
And set down that drink with the rest on the bar.

'There, that is for Harry,' he said, 'and it's queer,
'Tis the very same glass that he drank from last year;
His name's on the glass, you can read it like print,
He scratched it himself with an old bit of flint;
I remember his drink—it was always Three Star'—
And the landlord looked out through the door of the bar.

He looked at the horses, and counted but three:
'You were always together—where's Harry?' cried he.
Oh, sadly they looked at the glass as they said,
'You may put it away, for our old mate is dead;'
But one, gazing out o'er the ridges afar, said,
'We owe him a shout—leave the glass on the bar.'

They thought of the far-away grave on the plain,
They thought of the comrade who came not again,
They lifted their glasses, and sadly they said:
'We drink to the name of the mate who is dead.'
And the sunlight streamed in, and a light like a star
Seemed to glow in the depth of the glass on the bar.

And still in that shanty a tumbler is seen,
It stands by the clock, always polished and clean;
And often the strangers will read as they pass
The name of a bushman engraved on the glass;
And though on the shelf but a dozen there are,
That glass never stands with the rest on the bar.

Henry Lawson, 1867 - 1922

W. H. Davies, 1871 – 1940

William Henry Davies was born in Newport, Monmouthshire. After his father's death, Davies was brought up by his grandparents. On leaving home, he travelled widely as a tramp or hobo in America. In 1899, he was keen to join the Klondike Gold Rush but he fell under the wheels of a train as he tried to jump aboard and his leg was crushed. Now unable to lead a life of adventure, Davies returned to Britain and began to compose poems in his head, writing them down when he had time to himself. He borrowed money to publish his first book of poems in 1905. Davies's best known poem, 'Leisure,' was part of this first collection.

Leisure

WHAT is this life if, full of care,
We have no time to stand and stare?—

No time to stand beneath the boughs,
And stare as long as sheep and cows:

No time to see, when woods we pass,
Where squirrels hide their nuts in grass:

No time to see, in broad daylight,
Streams full of stars, like skies at night:

No time to turn at Beauty's glance,
And watch her feet, how they can dance:

No time to wait till her mouth can
Enrich that smile her eyes began?

A poor life this if, full of care,
We have no time to stand and stare.

W. H. Davies, 1871 - 1940

Paul Laurence Dunbar, 1872 – 1906

Dunbar was born in Dayton, Ohio, just a few years after the end of the American Civil War. Until slavery was abolished in 1865, his mother had been a slave in Kentucky. His father escaped slavery during the Civil War and fought for the Union. Dunbar was the only African-American at Central High School, where he was elected president of the school's literary society and became editor of the school magazine. On leaving school Dunbar took a job as an elevator operator (or lift attendant), and used the money he earned to help publish his first book of poems in 1892. In a brief career he published twelve books of poems on many subjects. He was diagnosed with tuberculosis in 1900, and died six years later.

Although slavery was officially abolished in 1865, attitudes did not change so quickly. Dunbar's poem 'Sympathy' compares the life of oppressed African-Americans with the life of a caged bird.

Sympathy

I KNOW what the caged bird feels, alas!
    When the sun is bright on the upland slopes;
When the wind stirs soft through the springing grass,
And the river flows like a stream of glass;
    When the first bird sings and the first bud opes,
And the faint perfume from its chalice steals—
I know what the caged bird feels!

I know why the caged bird beats his wing
    Till its blood is red on the cruel bars;
For he must fly back to his perch and cling
When he fain would be on the bough a-swing;
    And a pain still throbs in the old, old scars
And they pulse again with a keener sting—
I know why he beats his wing!

I know why the caged bird sings, ah me,
    When his wing is bruised and his bosom sore—
When he beats his bars and he would be free;
It is not a carol of joy or glee,
    But a prayer that he sends from his heart's deep core,
But a plea, that upward to Heaven he flings—
I know why the caged bird sings!

Paul Laurence Dunbar, 1872 - 1906

Edward Thomas, 1878 – 1917

Philip Edward Thomas was born in Lambeth, and went to Battersea Grammar School, St Paul's School, and to Oxford University. He married in 1899 while still studying at university, and began to work as a book reviewer. He saw poetry as the highest form of writing, but only began to write his own poetry in 1914. In 1915, he enlisted in the British Army to fight in the First World War becoming Second Lieutenant in the Royal Garrison Artilley in October 1916. He was killed by a shell in the aftermath of the Battle of Arras.

In June 1914, Thomas had been visiting poet friends in Gloucestershire, when his train unexpectedly stopped at Adlestrop. This poem was probably written later that year.

Adlestrop

YES. I remember Adlestrop—
The name, because one afternoon
Of heat the express-train drew up there
Unwontedly. It was late June.

The steam hissed. Someone cleared his throat.
No one left and no one came
On the bare platform. What I saw
Was Adlestrop—only the name

And willows, willow-herb, and grass,
And meadowsweet, and haycocks dry,
No whit less still and lonely fair
Than the high cloudlets in the sky.

And for that minute a blackbird sang
Close by, and round him, mistier,
Farther and farther, all the birds
Of Oxfordshire and Gloucestershire.

Edward Thomas, 1878 - 1917

James Elroy Flecker, 1884 – 1915

James Elroy Flecker was born in Lewisham, London. He went to school in Cheltenham, Gloucestershire, and Uppingham, Rutland, and he studied at both Oxford and Cambridge Universities. From 1910, Flecker worked as a British diplomat in Istanbul, Smyrna and Beirut. He became ill with tuberculosis and, in 1913 he went to Switzerland where he died two years later at the age of 30.

Flecker was seen as an important poet in his own lifetime, and 'The Old Ships' is among his most popular poems. In Flecker's day, old wooden boats were a common sight on the Mediterranean. As a poet, Flecker was very much aware that he was living and working in the region where the heroes of the Trojan War had sailed four thousand years before, as described by the Ancient Greek poet Homer.

the village which men still call Tyre: *Tyros in Arcadia, Greece; Tyre is also the name of a major port in Lebanon.*
Famagusta: *a medieval port on Cyprus.*
The pirate Genoese: *Genoa was among many small independent states whose sailors sometimes acted more-or-less as pirates.*
Ææa: *a mythical island where Odysseus is said to have visited the sorceress Circe on his long return voyage from Troy.*

The Old Ships

I HAVE seen old ships sail like swans asleep
Beyond the village which men still call Tyre,
With leaden age o'ercargoed, dipping deep
For Famagusta and the hidden sun
That rings black Cyprus with a lake of fire;
And all those ships were certainly so old—
Who knows how oft with squat and noisy gun,
Questing brown slaves or Syrian oranges,
The pirate Genoese
Hell-raked them till they rolled
Blood, water, fruit and corpses up the hold.
But now through friendly seas they softly run,
Painted the mid-sea blue or shore-sea green,
Still patterned with the vine and grapes in gold.

But I have seen,
Pointing her shapely shadows from the dawn
An image tumbled on a rose-swept bay,
A drowsy ship of some yet older day;
And, wonder's breath indrawn,
Thought I—who knows—who knows—but in that same
(Fished up beyond Aeaea, patched up new
—Stern painted brighter blue—)
That talkative, bald-headed seaman came
(Twelve patient comrades sweating at the oar)
From Troy's doom-crimson shore,
And with great lies about his wooden horse
Set the crew laughing, and forgot his course.

It was so old a ship—who knows, who knows?
—And yet so beautiful, I watched in vain
To see the mast burst open with a rose,
And the whole deck put on its leaves again.

James Elroy Flecker, 1884 - 1915

Rupert Brooke, 1887 – 1915

Rupert Brooke was born in Rugby, Warwickshire, where his father was a schoolmaster. He won a scholarship to Cambridge University. By the time war broke out in 1914, he was already well known as a poet. One of his most famous poems describes his home in Grantchester, Cambridgeshire. Brooke joined the Royal Naval Reserve in 1914 and took part in the Antwerp Expedition later that year. In 1915 he sailed with the fleet for Gallipolli, but died en route from blood poisoning following an insect bite, and was buried on the island of Skyros, Greece.

Brooke's poem 'The Soldier' tells of a young soldier facing up to the possibility of death on the battlefield. 'The Soldier' was a famous poem from its first publication, and was read aloud by the Dean of St Paul's Cathedral, London, for Easter Sunday 1915.

The Soldier

IF I should die, think only this of me:
That there's some corner of a foreign field
That is forever England. There shall be
In that rich earth a richer dust concealed;
A dust whom England bore, shaped, made aware,
Gave, once, her flowers to love, her ways to roam,
A body of England's, breathing English air,
Washed by the rivers, blest by the suns of home.
And think, this heart, all evil shed away,
A pulse in the eternal mind, no less
Gives somewhere back the thoughts by England given;
Her sights and sounds; dreams happy as her day;
And laughter, learnt of friends; and gentleness,
In hearts at peace, under an English heaven.

Rupert Brooke, 1887 - 1915

Wilfred Owen, 1893 – 1918

Wilfred Owen was born near Oswestry in Shropshire. His family moved several times when he was a child. He did well at school, but was too poor to go to university. When he was 19, he began work in Bordeaux, France, teaching English and French. In 1915 he joined the army to fight in the First World War, and became a Second Lieutenant in the Manchester Regiment serving in the trenches of the Western Front. Wilfred Owen was killed in action just one week before the end of the war. He was 25 years old. After his death, he was awarded the Military Cross 'for conspicuous gallantry and devotion to duty.'

Owen's poem 'Futility' expresses the pain and anger he felt at the terrible loss of life in the First World War, as well as his feeling of tenderness towards the fallen soldier. Wilfred Owen's poems were not published in his lifetime but he was planning a book of poems before his death. His Preface says, 'This book is not about heroes ... My subject is War, and the pity of War. The Poetry is in the pity.'

Futility

MOVE him into the sun—
Gently its touch awoke him once,
At home, whispering of fields half-sown.
Always it woke him, even in France,
Until this morning and this snow.
If anything might rouse him now
The kind old sun will know.

Think how it wakes the seeds,—
Woke, once, the clays of a cold star.
Are limbs, so dear-achieved, are sides,
Full-nerved—still warm—too hard to stir?
Was it for this the clay grew tall?
—O what made fatuous sunbeams toil
To break earth's sleep at all?

Wilfred Owen, 1893 - 1918

www.ingramcontent.com/pod-product-compliance
Lightning Source LLC
LaVergne TN
LVHW091109080426
835508LV00009B/891